FIRST FIELD GUIDE TO BUTTERFLIES & MOTHS
OF SOUTHERN AFRICA

SIMON VAN NOORT

Contents

Introduction	3
Grouping butterflies and moths	4
Butterfly or moth?	6
Collecting butterflies and moths	7
Rearing butterflies and moths	8
How to use this book	9
Butterfly descriptions	10
Moth descriptions	30
Glossary	54
Recommended further reading	55
Index and checklist	56
Acknowledgements and photographic credits	57

Slug Moth, *Latoia vivida*

Published by Struik Nature
(an imprint of Penguin Random House (Pty) Ltd
Reg. No. 1953/000441/07
The Estuaries No 4, Oxbow Crescent,
Century Avenue, Century City, 7441
PO Box 1144, Cape Town, 8000 South Africa

Visit **www.penguinrandomhouse.co.za** and join the Struik Nature Club for updates, news, events and special offers.

Copyright © in published edition, 1999:
Penguin Random House (Pty) Ltd
Copyright © in illustrations, 1999:
Penguin Random House (Pty) Ltd
Copyright © in text, 1999: Simon Van Noort
Copyright © in photographs, 1999:
as credited on page 57

First published in 1999
10

All rights reserved. No part of this publication may be reproduced, stored in a retrieval system or transmitted, in any form or by any means, electronic, mechanical, photocopying, recording or otherwise, without the prior written permission of the copyright holders.

Editor: Gary Lyon
Designer: Dominic Robson
Proofreader: Cara Cilliers
Concept designer: Petal Palmer

Reproduction by Disc Express Cape (Pty) Ltd.
Printed and bound by Times Offset (M)
Sdn Bhd, Malaysia

ISBN 978 1 86872 287 7

Introduction

Butterflies and moths are among the best known and most visible insects. They are one of 32 different orders of insects and belong to a group known as Lepidoptera, which is the second largest insect order, after the beetles, with approximately 170 000 known species worldwide. Ninety per cent of this total are moths. The term Lepidoptera means 'scaly wings' and refers to the thousands of tiny overlapping scales that cover the wings and bodies of these creatures. The scales provide the colour and patterns of the wings, and are easily rubbed off, leaving a transparent membrane with a network of veins.

Butterflies and moths have a wide range of colours, forms and sizes. Size ranges from moths with a wingspan of a couple of millimetres to giants with a wingspan of 30 centimetres. Southern Africa is home to the Dwarf Blue, one of the smallest butterflies in the world, and the smallest in Africa. Our largest butterfly, the Emperor Swallowtail, has a wingspan of up to 12,5 cm; some of our Emperor Moths have wingspans as wide as 18 cm.

Many adult butterflies and moths are important pollinators of a wide variety of plants. Butterflies visit flowers to feed on nectar, which they suck up with a modified mouthpart – their long hollow tongue (proboscis). When not feeding, this tongue is coiled up beneath the head. During feeding, pollen sticks to the butterfly's body and is carried from one flower to another, resulting in cross-pollination of the flowers.

Snouted Tiger Moth, *Psephea speciosa*

Butterflies and moths consume most of their food during the caterpillar stage. Nectar is, however, needed by the adults to provide energy for flight (although a number of moths do not feed at all in the adult stage and as a result are shortlived). Caterpillars are 'eating machines' and consume vast quantities of plant material. They play an important part in food chains by converting leaves into protein (themselves). Caterpillars are then eaten by many other life forms, including insects, spiders, birds and lizards.

Grouping butterflies and moths

All living things are grouped according to shared characteristics in a logical system of classification. Animals are grouped together in the *Kingdom* Animalia, which is divided into a number of smaller groups each called a *Phylum*. One such group is the phylum Arthropoda, which includes crabs, spiders, and insects. Each of these

Handmaiden, *Syntomis cerbera*

groups is, in turn, known as a *Class*. Butterflies and moths belong to the insect class Hexapoda. The class Hexapoda, in turn, contains a number of *orders*, one of which is the Lepidoptera (butterflies and moths). The order Lepidoptera includes 30 *superfamilies*. The Butterflies are grouped together in the superfamilies Papilionoidea and Hesperioidea. The remaining 28 superfamilies are all moths. Superfamilies are divided into *families*, which in turn are divided into *subfamilies*. Subfamilies contain *genera* (singular genus), which are made up of a number of related species. A species is one particular kind of butterfly or moth. For example the Christmas Swallowtail is classified as follows:

Habitats

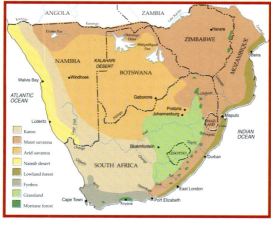

Regions

Kingdom	Animalia
Phylum	Arthropoda
Class	Hexapoda
Order	Lepidoptera
Superfamily	Papilionoidea
Family	Papilionidae
Subfamily	Papilioninae
Genus	*Papilio*
Species	*demodocus*

The scientific name of the Christmas Swallowtail is thus *Papilio demodocus* and is always written in italics.

Butterfly or moth?

Butterflies should not really be separated from moths, since butterflies form a natural group contained within the larger group of moths. Moths tend to be more drab and are active at night (nocturnal), whereas what we call butterflies are mostly very colourful and are active during the day (diurnal). However, many moths are just as colourful as butterflies and a good number are also active during the day.

The following combination of characters is useful in distinguishing moths from butterflies.

Moths mostly have either feathery, or slender and smooth antennae which taper to a point.
Butterflies have clubbed antennae, or in the case of the Skippers, a thickening towards the end of the feeler which has a slight hook.

Moths have a hook and catch mechanism that joins the fore- and hindwings together.
Butterflies lack this joining apparatus, with the exception of some of the Skippers.

Moths either rest with their wings spread out flat on either side of the body or fold their wings in a roof-like manner over the abdomen[G].
Butterflies usually rest with their wings closed together in an upright position above the body, although some Skippers rest with their wings spread flat.

Collecting butterflies and moths

Butterflies and moths can be found almost anywhere, and a good place to start looking is in your own back garden. The warmer summer months are the best time of the year to collect butterflies and moths because that is when they are most active. The northeastern region of southern Africa is, however, warm enough throughout the year to catch moths and butterflies.

To catch the faster flying butterflies you will need to make a collecting net, but many moths can be hand-picked off walls at night where they have been attracted to light. Be careful not to touch the wings, for this will remove the scales and therefore the colours and patterns. It is also not a good idea to keep butterflies or moths in a jar or container as they will quickly damage their wings by flapping around inside.

To make a preserved collection, you will need to stun larger butterflies or moths with a quick pinch to the thorax[G] with the thumb and forefinger. Place the specimen in an envelope and leave it in the freezer overnight. Smaller specimens can be placed directly in the freezer or killed with ethyl acetate. The butterfly or moth will then have to be set and dried in the standard way, with the wings spread out on either side. The method for this is detailed in a number of books listed under 'Recommended further reading' on page 55. Try not to collect more than one or two representatives of each species, and do not collect threatened species (listed in the *Red Data Book* on Butterflies). Over-collecting, however, is rarely responsible for the decline in butterfly or moth numbers; the real culprit is the large-scale destruction of their habitats.

Chrysalis of *Graphium antheus*

Rearing butterflies and moths

Butterflies and moths go through a complete change (metamorphosis[G]) during their life cycle, which has four distinct stages: egg, caterpillar (larva), chrysalis[G] (pupa) and finally the adult (see below). The first three stages (called immature) can be found on the food plants of butterflies and moths. Knowing your plants can be handy when searching for the immature stages of a particular species; however there are not many plants that escape the attention of caterpillars, and with careful observation you should soon locate specimens.

Once found, the eggs or caterpillars can be placed together with their food plant in a suitable plastic container or specially constructed cage. You will need to provide fresh leaves each day to rear the caterpillars through to the adult stage. The life cycles of many species have not yet been worked out, so it is a good idea to record your observations and the details of food plants and length of development for each stage. *'A Practical Guide to the Butterflies and Moths in Southern Africa'* (Woodhall) has useful information on rearing.

Stages in the life cycle of the Hawk Moth, *Theretra capensis*

How to use this book

This book introduces the reader to the more common moth and butterfly *groups,* (rather than individual species), that occur in the southern African region.

Names Each account gives the group's **common name**, the *representative* **genera** (singular: genus) and the **family name**.

Average size Gives the wingspan of the adult in centimetres.

Identification Each description outlines the main diagnostic features of the butterflies or moths in a group.

Distribution The number of species in each group and their distribution in the region are given.

Behaviour The feeding and territorial habits, and flight patterns are explained.

Early stages Brief descriptions are given of the various stages in the life cycle of the moth or butterfly from the egg through to the adult.

Food Gives the plant families on which the caterpillars feed.

Notes Reference is made to one or more interesting species that occur in a family.

Similar species or groups are brought to the attention of the reader.

Where technical terms are used they appear with a small [G], which indicates that they are defined in the Glossary on page 54.

Caterpillar of *Papilio demodocus*

Swallowtail Butterflies

Papilio

Family: Papilionidae.

Average size: 9 cm wingspan.

Identification: Wings are large and showy; often with tails on the hindwing. Male and female are usually similar in appearance.

Papilio demodocus

Distribution: Six of the species occurring in the region are restricted to the eastern parts of southern Africa. The Christmas Swallowtail (*Papilio demodocus*) is widespread throughout the region.

Behaviour: They are strong fliers, and typically stop to feed at flowers; they often gather on mud to drink water. Males patrol territories such as hill tops, or forest streams.

Early stages: Eggs are laid singly on leaves. Young caterpillars are black and white and resemble bird-droppings. Older caterpillars are usually green and black. A bright-orange, forked fleshy process (used to deter predators) is pushed out above the head. The caterpillar moults in five separate growth stages over a period of four to five weeks. The chrysalis[G] is angular and either brown or green; attached by the tail end in an upright position. Adults emerge after two to three weeks.

Food: Commonly plants in the Citrus family.

Notes: The Emperor Swallowtail (*Papilio ophidicephalus*) is the largest southern African butterfly with a wingspan of 12,5 cm. The Bush-Kite Swallowtail (*Papilio euphranor*) is endemic[G] to South Africa.

Similar species: Swordtail Butterflies (*Graphium*).

Swordtail Butterflies

Graphium

Family: Papilionidae.

Average size: 6 cm wingspan.

Identification: Smaller than Swallowtails, often with a sword-shaped tail on the hindwing. Male and female are similar in appearance.

Distribution: All 10 species occurring in the region are restricted to the northeastern parts of southern Africa.

Behaviour: They are strong fliers and stop only to feed at flowers; they often gather on mud to drink water. Males patrol territories such as hill tops.

Early stages: Eggs are laid singly on leaves. Young caterpillars usually have black and yellow stripes. Older caterpillars are green, yellow or black; six sharp projections protrude from the front region and two at the tail end. The caterpillar moults in five separate growth stages over a period of two to three weeks. The chrysalis[G] is angular, either brown or green; attached by the tail end in an upright position. Adults emerge after one week, but may take longer under unfavourable conditions.

Food: Commonly plants in the Custard Apple family.

Notes: The Small White-Lady Swordtail (*Graphium morania*) is endemic[G] to southern Africa.

Similar species: Swallowtail Butterflies (*Papilio*).

Graphium antheus

White Butterflies

Appias, Belenois, Dixeia, Leptosia, Pontia and others

Family: Pieridae.

Average size: 5 cm wingspan.

Identification: Wings are white or yellow, with irregular black or brown borders.

Distribution: The Brown-veined White (*Belenois aurota*) and Meadow White (*Pontia helice*) are widespread. The remaining 13 species occurring in the region are restricted to the eastern or north-eastern parts of southern Africa.

Behaviour: The Brown-veined White sets out on mass summer migrations in a north-easterly direction in southern Africa. Males of most species have a fast flight. Females fly more slowly looking for food plants on which to lay eggs.

Early stages: Eggs are yellow or red and are laid singly. The caterpillars are variable in colour; most are green, often with yellow stripes; they have stiff hairs along the sides of the body and around the head. The caterpillar moults in five separate growth stages over a period of four weeks. The chrysalis[G] is either brown or green, with a blunt spine at the top and on each side of the chrysalis[G]; attached by the tail end in an upright position. Adults emerge after two weeks.

Food: Commonly plants in the Caper family.

Notes: Spines on the chrysalis[G] mimic[G] spines on the host plant, which provides camouflage.

Similar species: False Dotted Border White (*Belenois thysa*) mimics[G] species of Dotted Borders (*Mylothris*).

Belenois aurota

12

Vagrant Butterflies

Eronia, Nepheronia

Family: Pieridae.

Average size: 5,5 cm wingspan.

Identification: Wings either cream with black borders, or yellow with a large orange tip.

Distribution: All six species occurring in the region are restricted to the northeastern side of southern Africa.

Behaviour: They are fast flyers, and stop only to feed at flowers and on damp ground.

Early stages: Eggs are elongate and laid singly. Young caterpillars are variable in colour; older caterpillars are green. The chrysalis[G] is green with strongly keeled[G] wing cases[G]; attached by the tail end at right angles to a plant stem, so resembling a leaf.

Food: Plants in the Caper, Mustard, Onionwood, Spike-thorn and Olive families.

Eronia cleodora

Notes: Underside of wings may resemble dried leaves, camouflaging the butterfly when at rest.

Similar species: The Autumn-leaf Vagrant (*Eronia leda*) resembles some of the smaller and weaker flying Orange Tips (*Colotis*). Buquet's Vagrant (*Nepheronia buquetii*) is similar to the African Migrant (*Catopsilia florella*), which has a dark spot in the middle of each forewing.

13

Grass Yellow Butterflies

Eurema

Family: Pieridae.

Average size: 4 cm wingspan.

Identification: Wings are yellow with black borders.

Distribution: The Broad-bordered Grass Yellow (*Eurema brigitta*) occurs throughout southern Africa except for the western side. Two species are restricted to the northeastern parts of southern Africa; the remaining two species occur in forested areas in Zimbabwe and Mozambique.

Behaviour: These are weak flyers, and often congregate to feed on damp ground.

Early stages: Eggs are elongate. Young caterpillars are yellow or white in colour; older caterpillars are green in colour with pale stripes along the length of the body. The chrysalis[G] is green and narrow with pointed ends; attached by the tail end in an upright position.

Eurema brigitta

Notes: The black border on the wings is wider in wet season specimens as opposed to those that appear in the dry season.

Food: Plants in the Bauhinia, Pea and Mangosteen families.

Similar species: Sulpher Small White (*Dixeia spilleri*), which has a narrow dark tip on the forewing.

Orange or Purple Tip Butterflies

Colotis

Family: Pieridae.

Average size: 4 cm wingspan.

Identification: Wings are white with black markings and orange or purple tips on the forewings.

Distribution: Many of the 19 species occurring in the region are restricted to the northeastern parts of southern Africa; a number favour drier habitats in the central or western parts of the region.

Behaviour: Generally fly slowly, close to the ground; but fly rapidly on disturbance. They feed at flowers and congregate on damp ground. Males patrol territories near their food plants.

Early stages: Eggs are usually laid singly. Young caterpillars are yellow or green in colour; older caterpillars are green and often have pale stripes. The chrysalis^G is green or brown and narrow with pointed ends, and has a pronounced keel^G on the wing cases^G. The chrysalis is attached by the tail end in an upright position.

Food: Many plants in the Caper family.

Notes: The black wing-markings vary and are lighter in the dry season; the female has darker markings than the male.

Similar species: The Sulpher Orange Tip (*Colotis auxo*) is similar to the much larger Autumn-leaf Vagrant (*Eronia leda*).

Colotis antevippe

Acraea Butterflies

Acraea, Bematistes, Hyalites, Pardopsis

Family: Nymphalidae (subfamily: Acraeinae).

Average size: 4-5 cm wingspan.

Identification: Wings are generally brick-red, yellow or white with black borders; often with scattered black dots.

Distribution: Most of the 50 species occurring in the region are restricted to the eastern or northeastern parts of southern Africa.

Behaviour: They usually have a slow, floating flight. Forest species tend to fly around the tree canopy; savanna species range more widely.

Early stages: Eggs are yellow and laid in clusters. The caterpillars are black, often with some orange, and covered with stiff, branched spines. The chrysalis[G] is black, chequered orange or yellow; attached by the tail end, it hangs in a downward position.

Food: Plants in families including the Granadilla, Wild Peach and Nettle among others.

Notes: The bright brick-red and black colours warn predators that these butterflies are distasteful.

Similar species: A number of Brush-footed Butterflies (subfamily Nymphalinae) mimic[G] Acraeas.

Acraea horta

16

Monarch Butterflies

Amauris, Danaus, Tirumala

Family: Nymphalidae (subfamily: Danainae).

Average size: 7 cm wingspan.

Identification: Wings are orange with black borders or are black with white or yellow patches.

Distribution: The African Monarch (*Danaus chrysippus*) is widespread throughout southern Africa. The remaining six species are restricted to the northeastern parts of the region.

Behaviour: All species have a slow, floating flight.

Early stages: Eggs are laid singly. The caterpillars are smooth with black and yellow bands; fleshy projections grow from the head and back. The chrysalis[G] is barrel-shaped, often with metallic gold patches; attached by the tail end, it hangs in a downward position.

Food: Plants in the Milkweed family.

Danaus chrysippus

Notes: Bright colours warn predators that they are distasteful. Caterpillars absorb poisons from their food plant.

Similar species: A number of Acraea, Brush-footed and Swallowtail Butterflies mimic[G] the Monarchs.

Brown Butterflies

Aeropetes, Bicyclus, Dira, Pseudonympha, Ypthima and others

Family: Nymphalidae (subfamily: Satyrinae).

Average size: 4-5 cm wingspan.

Identification: Wings are generally brown with red patches and black and white eyespots; a few of the Browns have yellow or white markings.

Distribution: Many of the 82 species occurring in the region have a localised distribution and are confined to the southwestern Cape or to highland grassland areas in the eastern parts of southern Africa. The remainder are widely distributed in the north-eastern parts of southern Africa.

Behaviour: Most species have a slow, flitting flight, often resting in shade; a few are strong, fast flyers.

Early stages: Eggs are sometimes scattered in flight. The caterpillar is smooth, with an angular head; the tail end has two projections. The chrysalis[G] is round; usually

Pseudonympha trimenii

attached by the tail end in a downward position, it may lie free on the ground.

Food: Plants in the Grass family.

Notes: There are 22 genera of Browns. Some of the more common genera are listed above. Evening Browns (*Melanitis*) usually fly at dusk.

Similar species: The Bush Beauty (*Paralethe dendrophilus*) is similar in colour to the African Monarch, which it may mimic[G].

Brush-footed Butterflies

Precis, Hypolimnas, Vanessa, Catacroptera and others

Family: Nymphalidae (subfamily: Nymphalinae).

Average size: 5-8 cm wingspan.

Identification: Robust, often colourful butterflies. Forewing often with an angular projection on the edge below the tip.

Distribution: A number of the 70 species occurring in the region are widespread, though most are restricted to the northeastern parts of southern Africa.

Behaviour: They are strong, fast flyers, beating their wings a few times before gliding for a stretch.

Early stages: Eggs are usually laid singly. The caterpillar often has rows of barbed spines, but may be smooth. The chrysalis[G] is angular, usually green; attached by the tail end, hanging head downwards.

Food: A wide range of plant families including the Wild Peach, Milkwood, Euphorbia, Combretum, Pea, Mint, Acanthus and Nettle.

Notes: The male and female of the Common Diadem (*Hypolimnas misippus*) are completely different in appearance. The Gaudy Commodore (*Junonia octavia sesamus*) varies in colour according to the season. There are 28 genera of Brush-footed Butterflies.

Similar species: A number of species mimic[G] the distasteful Monarch and Acraea Butterflies.

Vanessa cardui

Charaxes Butterflies

Charaxes, Euxanthe

Family: Nymphalidae (subfamily: Charaxinae).

Average size: 6-7 cm wingspan.

Identification: Large, heavy-bodied, colourful butterflies, most with two short tails on each hindwing.

Distribution: Most of the 38 species occurring in the region are restricted to the northeastern parts of southern Africa.

Behaviour: They are strong, fast flyers. Adults feed on carnivore dung, tree sap and fermenting fruit. The male uses the serrated edge on its forewing to jostle other males at feeding sites.

Early stages: Eggs are laid singly. The caterpillar is smooth, tapering towards the tail end; the head is shield-like with projecting horns. The chrysalis[G] is round with a pointed head; attached by the tail end, it hangs head downwards.

Charaxes varanes

Food: A wide range of plant families, including the Litchi, Euphorbia, and Pea families.

Notes: Male and female are often completely different in appearance; others, such as the Club-tailed Charaxes (*Charaxes zoolina zoolina*), vary in colour according to the season.

Similar species: Most Charaxes are distinct butterflies and do not resemble any other groups. However, the Forest Queen (*Euxanthe wakefieldi*) resembles some Monarch and Brush-footed Butterflies (subfamilies Danainae and Nymphalinae respectively).

Snout Butterflies

Libythea

Family: Nymphalidae (subfamily: Libytheinae).

Average size: 5 cm wingspan.

Identification: The wings are dark brown on the upperside with orange flecks and white marks on the forewing. Prominent palps[G] (snout) extend forward from the head, giving the butterfly its common name.

Distribution: The single species is restricted to the northeastern parts of southern Africa.

Libythea labdaca wings closed

Behaviour: They are fast flyers, often settling out of reach on twigs, but are also attracted to damp mud.

Early stages: Eggs are jar-shaped. The caterpillar is smooth with spines behind the head. The chrysalis[G] is angular; attached by the tail end, it hangs head downwards.

Food: Plants in the Elm family.

Notes: The African Snout (*Libythea labdaca laius*) is the only species of this family in southern Africa.

Similar species: The palps (snout) distinguish this butterfly.

Libythea labdaca wings open

Zulu Butterflies

Alaena

Family: Lycaenidae (subfamily: Lipteninae).

Average size: 2,5 cm wingspan.

Identification: Wings are orange with black-lined veins, or black with a white crescent patch on each wing.

Distribution: The four species occurring in the region are restricted to the northeastern parts of southern Africa.

Behaviour: They are weak flyers, flitting from one grass stem to another. They rest for long periods on these stems, where they are well camouflaged.

Early stages: Eggs are laid singly or in small clusters on or near lichen-covered rocks. Young caterpillars have very long hairs, older caterpillars have shorter bristles. The chrysalis[G] is bristly, attached to its partly discarded previous skin which in turn is attached to a rock.

Food: Algae on rocks.

Notes: Rather similar in appearance and behaviour to some day-flying moth species which they probably mimic[G].

Similar species: Clouded Orange (Looper Moths, Geometridae); Small Bordered Orange and Dusky Vapourer (Tussock Moths, Lymantriidae).

Alaena amazoula

Skolly Butterflies

Thestor

Family: Lycaenidae (subfamily: Miletinae).

Average size: 3,5 cm wingspan.

Identification: Wings are brown or yellowish-brown in colour with small black square patches. The wing edges are chequered dark brown and white.

Distribution: 26 of the 27 species occurring in the region are restricted to western South Africa; the Basuto Skolly (*Thestor basutus*) occurs in the northeastern parts of southern Africa.

Behaviour: They have a fast, short flight pattern, frequently settling on the ground.

Early stages: Eggs are laid singly or in small clusters, near ant nests, or on plants with scale and related insects. Young caterpillars are white with brownish-orange stripes and with long hairs at each end; older caterpillars are yellowish-brown with darker spots. The chrysalis[G] is smooth and brown, and rests on the floor in an ant nest.

Food: Young caterpillars feed on scale and related insects; older caterpillars live inside ant nests.

Notes: The species are difficult to tell apart, but each is isolated geographically from the others and one can identify them by the places in which they are found. The life cycle of most species is not known.

Similar species: Some of the Blues (*Lepidochrysops*), but these are distinguished by their distinct black spots seen on the underside of the hindwing, at the base.

Thestor protumnus

Sapphire Butterflies

Iolaus

Family: Lycaenidae (subfamily: Theclinae).

Average size: 3-3,5 cm wingspan.

Identification: Wings are blue (metallic in male), or white and blue with broad black tips to the forewing. The Saffron Sapphire (*Iolaus pallene*) is yellow. All species have a pair of long flimsy tails on each hindwing.

Distribution: The 21 species occurring in the region are restricted to the northeastern parts of southern Africa.

Behaviour: They have a short, fast flight, usually around trees or bushes, and frequently settle on twigs or leaves.

Early stages: Eggs are laid singly on a leaf or stem. Young caterpillars are pale with long hairs on each segment; older caterpillars are smooth, brown or green, and hump-shaped. The chrysalis[G] is

Iolaus silas

brown or green, often with uneven projections in the middle.

Food: Plants of the parasitic Mistletoe family.

Notes: Scientists sometimes split the genus *Iolaus* into a number of genera, including *Stugeta*, *Epamera* and *Argiolaus*.

Similar species: The closely related Hairstreaks (*Hypolycaena*).

Copper Butterflies

Aloeides, Argyraspodes, Trimenia, Tylopaedia

Family: Lycaenidae (subfamily: Theclinae).

Average size: 3 cm wingspan.

Identification: Wings are orange with black or brown borders, and small white, black-ringed spots on the underside of the forewing.

Distribution: Most of the 60 species occurring in the region have a localised distribution, many being restricted to the Western Cape. However, a few are more widespread in southern Africa.

Behaviour: They have a short, fast, erratic flight, frequently settling on the ground.

Early stages: Eggs are laid singly on low shrubs or on the ground. Young caterpillars are pale with long hairs on each segment; older caterpillars are brown or green, with short hairs; the body tapers towards the tail end. The chrysalis[G] is brown

Aloeides sp.

or green and smooth, and is found under stones near its food plant.

Food: Plants in the Pea, Cacao, Hibiscus, Zygophyllum, Ebony and Buffalo-thorn families.

Notes: Older caterpillars of some species spend the day inside an ant nest, emerging to feed at night.

Similar species: Opal Butterflies which are distinguished by having numerous black markings and sometimes a violet sheen on the upperside of the wings.

Opal Butterflies

Chrysoritis

Family: Lycaenidae (subfamily: Theclinae).

Average size: 2,5 cm wingspan.

Identification: Wings are orange chequered with black, many showing a pearl and violet sheen at the wing bases; the hindwing has a stubby-pointed tail.

Distribution: Most of the 56 species occurring in the region have a localised distribution, many restricted to areas within the Western Cape in Southern Africa.

Behaviour: They are strong, fast flyers, frequently settling on the ground.

Early stages: Eggs are laid singly on leaves or stems. Young caterpillars are pale with long hairs on each segment; older caterpillars have brown or green stripes and short hairs; the body tapers towards the tail end. The chrysalis^G is brown or green and smooth, and develops in dried leaf-shelters.

Chrysoritis thysbe

Food: Plants in a number of families including the Daisy, Mango, Crassula, Pea and Zygophyllum.

Notes: The caterpillars are attended by ants, and often rest in shelters made from joined leaves.

Similar species: Copper Butterflies, which are distinguished by plain uppersides to the wing; Sorrel Copper Butterflies (*Lycaena*; subfamily Lycaeninae), which have rounder wing margins.

Hairtail Butterflies

Anthene

Family: Lycaenidae (subfamily: Polyommatinae).

Average size: 2,5-3 cm wingspan.

Identification: The male's wings are dark purple or brown; the female's wings are brown with purple or white patches on each wing and orange eyespots on the hindwing margin. Both sexes have three fine, short tails on each hindwing.

Distribution: Most of the 24 species occurring in the region are limited in distribution, restricted to areas in northeastern parts of the region. Some are more widespread, extending into the Cape in Southern Africa.

Behaviour: Males are brisk flyers, establishing territories around Acacia trees. Females fly more slowly and remain closer to the ground.

Early stages: Eggs are laid singly on leaves. Young caterpillars are

Anthene definata

pale with long hairs on each segment; older caterpillars are green with brown marks; the outline of segments from a side-on view creates a toothed appearance. The chrysalis^G is smooth, brown or green; attached by the tail end in an upright position.

Food: Plants of a number of families, but commonly the Pea family.

Notes: The caterpillars are attended by ants.

Similar species: Hairtails are distinguished from all other butterflies by the presence of three short tails on each hindwing.

Blue Butterflies

Azanus, Lampides, Lepidochrysops, Cacyreus and others

Family: Lycaenidae (subfamily: Polyommatinae).

Average size: 2,5-3 cm wingspan.

Identification: Wings are purple, blue or brown; some have orange eyespots and/or a single, fine tail on the hindwing.

Distribution: Many of the 123 species occurring in the region are widespread, others are more limited in distribution.

Behaviour: A few species are fast flyers; most flit around low vegetation. Some establish territories around Acacia tree tops.

Early stages: Eggs are laid singly on buds. Young caterpillars are pale in colour with long hairs on each segment; older caterpillars are green with brown marks, and taper towards the tail end. The chrysalis[G] is smooth, or has spiny hairs, and is brown or green; it is attached by the tail end in an upright position or develops inside ant nests.

Lampides boeticus

Food: Plants in a number of families including the Pea, Mint, Geranium, Buffalo-thorn, Plumbago and Selago.

Notes: Some caterpillars are either attended by ants on the food plant, or live inside ant nests. There are 24 genera of Blue Butterflies.

Similar species: Some species may be confused with the Skolly Butterflies (*Thestor*). A few are similar to the Hairtails (*Anthene*), which have three hindwing tails.

28

Skipper Butterflies

Borbo, Coeliades, Kedestes, Metisella, Platylesches and others

Family: Hesperiidae.

Average size: 3 cm wingspan.

Identification: Wings are brown with yellow or white markings; they have broad bodies; the feelers are curved or hooked at their ends.

Distribution: A number of the 136 species occurring in the region are widespread; however, most are restricted to the eastern or north-eastern parts of southern Africa.

Behaviour: They have a fast, darting flight, frequently settling on vegetation or on the ground. Males patrol territories on hill tops.

Early stages: Eggs are laid singly. The caterpillars have large heads, and may be brightly coloured; however most are brown or green. They often spin leaves together to create a shelter. The chrysalis[G] is brown or green, smooth, elongate and usually pointed at both ends; it develops in a leaf shelter, or a light cocoon.

Metisella metis

Food: Plants in a wide range of families; many species feed on grasses.

Notes: A few species fly at dusk. Skippers are represented by 31 genera.

Similar species: Skippers are moth-like in appearance. A few genera resemble the Looper Moths (family Geometridae).

Ghost Moths

Afrotheora, Eudalaca, Gorgopis, Leto, Metahepialus and others

Family: Hepialidae.

Average size: 4 cm wingspan.

Identification: Wings are mostly drab brown or yellow. The Silver Spotted Ghost (*Leto venus*) has orange-brown wings with silver markings on the forewing. All have large abdomens, short feelers, long narrow wings and hind- and forewings that are similar in size.

Silver Spotted Ghost, *Leto venus*

Distribution: The Silver Spotted Ghost is restricted to the south-western Cape; the 67 other species occurring in the region are more widespread in southern Africa.

Behaviour: The short-lived Silver Spotted Ghosts are weak flyers and nocturnal[G]; other genera have a faster flight.

Early stages: Eggs are scattered in flight or laid in the ground at the base of the food plant. The caterpillar is long, cylindrical, and pale in colour with darker patches. The chrysalis[G] is elongate, and may have spines on the abdominal segments, it develops in a tunnel bored by the caterpillar, or in an underground cocoon.

Food: Silver Spotted Ghosts bore into Keurboom trees; other genera feed on plant roots.

Notes: These are primitive moths.

Similar species: The Silver Spotted Ghost is distinctive; the remaining species may be confused with the Goat Moths (family Cossidae).

Bagworm Moths

Eumeta, Kotochalia, Melasina, Monda, Psyche and others

Family: Psychidae.

Average size: 2-3 cm wingspan.

Identification: The female moth may be wingless and grub-like, without mouth parts or feelers, and then remains in a bag made of silk and debris. The male's and some female's wings are either pale brown and cream, or transparent.

Distribution: Many of the 150 species occurring in the region are widespread; others are restricted to the northeastern parts of southern Africa.

Behaviour: Most genera are nocturnal[G]; species of *Monda* are diurnal[G]. The male may mate with the female inside her silk and debris bag, in which she then lays her eggs and dies.

Early stages: Eggs are laid in clusters. The bag is a silk-lined case constructed from twigs, thorns, grass or leaves. The caterpillars make new bags as they grow. The chrysalis[G] is brown and elongate, and develops inside the bag.

Food: Thorn-tree family, and Lichens.

Notes: One species is a pest in Wattle plantations. Bagworm Moths are represented by 46 genera.

Similar species: Species in several other families also construct bags, among them Goat Moths (family Cossidae). Processionary Moths (family Thaumetopidae) construct communal bag nests.

Kotochalia sp.

Clothes Moths

Amydria, Ceratophaga, Monopis, Tinea, Tineola and others

Family: Tineidae.

Average size: 2 cm wingspan.

Identification: Wings are often cream or orange-brown, either mottled or with spots; the wings are narrow, the hindwings fringed with hairs. The feelers are relatively long.

Distribution: Some of the 200 species occurring in the region are widespread; most are restricted to the northeastern parts of southern Africa.

Behaviour: Nocturnal[G]. The caterpillars of some species feed on woollen clothing and fabrics, rolling themselves into the material as they feed. Other species of this group bore into animal horn or hide, on which they feed.

Early stages: The caterpillars are pale in colour and smooth. The chrysalis[G] forms in a silk cocoon or inside horn or hide, excreting chimney-like structures when the adult emerges to leave.

Food: Many species feed on debris in old bird or rat nests; the Horn moth (*Ceratophaga vastella*) feeds on old antelope horn or hide.

Notes: Only very few species actually feed on clothes or carpets. The family contains 77 genera.

Ceratophaga vastella

Similar species: Web Spinners (family Yponomeutidae), but these have strong spots on the forewing. Some Pearl Moths (family Pyralidae) have a similar wing shape but lack the hindwing fringe.

Clearwing Moths

Chamanthedon, Homogyna, Melittia, Synanthedon and others

Family: Sesiidae.

Average size: 2,5 cm wingspan.

Identification: Wings are black and yellow or orange. Many have clear patches on the wings, some have hairy legs.

Distribution: Most of the approximately 61 described species occurring in the region are restricted to the northeastern parts of southern Africa.

Monopetalotaxis candescens

Behaviour: Diurnal[G], alert and swift flyers, sometimes settling on vegetation.

Early stages: The caterpillars are pale and smooth, and bore into the stems of trees or shrubs. The chrysalis[G] develops in one of the tunnels bored by the caterpillar and has hooks to enable movement within the tunnel.

Food: Poorly documented, but a southwestern Cape species bores into Protea stems.

Notes: The adults mimic[G] wasps and bees for protection against predators. The Clearwing Moth family is represented in southern Africa by 20 genera.

Similar species: Distinct from all other moths, Clearwing Moths are often mistaken for wasps or bees.

Goat Moths

Arctiocossus, Azygophleps, Coryphodema, Cossus and others

Family: Cossidae.

Average size: 7 cm wingspan.

Identification: The long narrow wings are usually brown with extensive white markings mottled with black. The abdomen is large, the feelers short.

Distribution: A few of the 100 or so described species occurring in the region are widespread; many are restricted to the northeastern parts of southern Africa.

Behaviour: Nocturnal[G], attracted to light.

Early stages: The caterpillar is pale with brown patches behind the head, and a long, cylindrical body; it bores into tree trunks. The chrysalis[G] is elongate, with spines on the abdominal segments; it develops in the tunnel bored by the caterpillar.

Food: Plants in the Cacao, Mahogany, Combretum, Bauhinia, Rose and Hibiscus families.

Azygophleps sp.

Notes: Some Goat Moth caterpillars inflict damage by boring into timber, and the wood of orchard and garden trees. The family contains 16 genera.

Similar species: May be confused with the Ghost Moths (family Hepialidae).

Burnet Moths

Callosymploca, Neurosymploca, Orna, Tascia and others

Family: Zygaenidae.

Average size: 2,5-3 cm wingspan.

Identification: Wings are mostly brightly coloured, black or greenish-black with either red, yellow or white spots, stripes or patches. The wings are long and narrow, the feelers prominent.

Distribution: Most of the approximately 48 described species occurring in the region are restricted to the northeastern parts of southern Africa, but a few occur only in the southwestern Cape.

Behaviour: Slow flyers; most are diurnal[G].

Early stages: The caterpillars are green or brown with darker markings, smooth, and have short hairs. The chrysalis[G] develops in a silk cocoon.

Neurosymploca sp.

Food: A number of plant families, including the Euphorbia, Protea and Grape families.

Notes: The bright colours of the adults warn predators that they are distasteful. The family contains 18 genera.

Similar species: Handmaidens (family Arctiidae, subfamily Ctenuchinae), but these usually have distinct, clear windows in the wings.

Leaf Rolling Moths

Ancylis, Bactra, Cydia, Eucosma, Tortrix and others

Family: Tortricidae.

Average size: 2,5 cm wingspan.

Identification: Wings are usually brown or orange with paler hindwings. The forewing has a distinct shape, with the leading edge curved outwards and the tip forming a blunt point.

Distribution: Many of the 250 or so described species occurring in the region are widespread throughout southern Africa.

Behaviour: The moths are nocturnal[G], and attracted to light. The caterpillars of many species roll themselves up in the leaves they feed on; some are leaf-miners or borers; others live in flowers.

Early stages: The caterpillars are pale cream or green in colour, with brown patches behind the head, and have short hairs. The chrysalis[G] develops in soil, in silken cocoons or between leaves that are spun together.

Food: Plants of the Citrus, Tomato, Carnation and Coffee families.

Notes: Sometimes a pest on Citrus and Coffee plants. The family contains 38 genera.

Similar species: The distinctive wing shape of this family distinguishes the Leaf Rollers from all other moth families.

Tortrix sp. with empty chrysalis[G]

Slug Moths

Coenobasis, Crothaema, Latoia, Natada, Taeda and others

Family: Limacodidae.

Average size: 3 cm wingspan.

Identification: Wings are often green and brown with paler hindwings, but can be yellow, brown or red. The moths usually have broad, rounded wings with short, robust, hairy bodies.

Distribution: Most of the approximately 105 species occurring in the region are restricted to the northeastern parts of southern Africa; some are widespread; a couple are restricted to the southwestern Cape.

Behaviour: Slug Moths include both diurnal[G] and nocturnal[G] species.

Early stages: The caterpillars are slug-like, often green with bright yellow, blue or orange markings. The body is smooth but is usually covered with groups of stinging hairs. The chrysalis[G] is contained in a brown, hard, egg-like cocoon.

Latoia latistriga

Food: A number of plants, including those in the Euphorbia, Waxberry, Ebony, Coffee and Rose families.

Notes: The bright colours of the caterpillars warn predators of the stinging hairs, which cause extreme pain, even to humans. The family comprises 52 genera.

Similar species: Some species are similar to the Eggar Moths (family Lasiocampidae).

Pearl Moths

Agrotera, Euclasta, Loxostege, Palpita, Pyrausta and others

Family: Pyralidae (subfamily: Pyraustinae).

Average size: 3 cm wingspan.

Identification: Wings are usually mottled brown or orange, a number are pure white; the forewing is narrower than the hindwing. The legs are long and slender.

Distribution: Most of the approximately 235 species occurring in the region are restricted to the northeastern parts of southern Africa; a number are widespread.

Behaviour: Adults rest flat on the undersides of leaves. Nocturnal[G], but often disturbed during the day.

Early stages: The caterpillars are cream or brown, sparsely covered with short hairs, and often feed in leaf shelters. The chrysalis[G] develops in white silken cocoons.

Food: Plants in a wide range of families, including the Fig, Grass, Acanthus, Hibiscus and Cabbage families.

Notes: The Pearl Moths are represented by 76 genera. The caterpillars often construct webbed shelters between leaves.

Similar species: Pearl Moths are distinctive, even from other groups within the family Pyralidae.

Pardomima sp.

Plume Moths

Buckleria, Marasmarcha, Platyptilia, Pterophorus and others

Family: Pterophoridae.

Average size: 2,5 cm wingspan.

Identification: These moths are delicate in appearance. The wings are grey or white, narrow, and divided into two or three plumes. The legs are long and thin.

Distribution: A few of the approximately 87 species occurring in the region are widespread throughout southern Africa, most are restricted to the northeastern parts.

Behaviour: Nocturnal[G], attracted to light.

Early stages: The caterpillar is green with a spiky shield on the head; the tail ends in spines.

Food: Plants in the Daisy family, among others.

Notes: The family contains 15 genera. The adults resemble mosquitoes when sitting on walls.

Similar species: The Many-Plumed Moths of the family Alucitidae, which have six or seven plumes on each wing.

Pterophorus callidus

39

Silk Moths

Ocinara

Family: Bombycidae.

Average size: 2,5 cm wingspan.

Identification: Wings are brown or grey, the hindwing concave on the inner margin, ending in a blunt projection. The body is broad and the feelers short.

Distribution: The four species are normally restricted to the north-eastern parts of southern Africa, but the Small Silk Moth (*Ocinara ficicola*) has been introduced into the southwestern Cape.

Behaviour: Adults are nocturnal[G]; the flight is weak and fluttering.

Early stages: Eggs are laid one on top of the other in stacks or columns. The caterpillars vary from brown and grey to green and yellow. The chrysalis[G] is contained in a tightly woven, yellow silk cocoon.

Food: Plants in the Fig family.

Notes: The caterpillars resemble twigs, which camouflages them from predators.

Similar species: Silk Moths are distinct and do not look like any other moths; they are, however, related to the much larger Emperor Moths (family Saturniidae).

Ocinara ficicola

Emperor Moths

Argema, Bunaea, Epiphora, Imbrasia, Ludia, Usta and others

Family: Saturniidae.

Average size: 10 cm wingspan.

Identification: Large, colourful moths with robust, hairy bodies, broad wings, and a large eyespot on each hindwing, sometimes also on the forewing. The feelers are short and feathery in the male.

Bunaea alcinoe

Distribution: A few of the 84 species occurring in the region are widespread; most are restricted to the northeastern parts of southern Africa.

Behaviour: Mostly nocturnal[G], attracted to light; a few species are diurnal[G]. The male uses feathery feelers to detect attractants released by the female.

Early stages: Eggs are laid in clusters. The caterpillars are large and fat, often with hairs or spines. The chrysalis[G] in most species develops in an earthen shell in the ground; a few spin a silk cocoon. The life cycle takes three months.

Food: Plants in a wide range of families but most commonly the Thorn-tree, Bauhinia, Myrrh and Mango families.

Notes: The family contains 31 genera. Adults do not feed and live for just three to four days. The caterpillars (Mopane worms) of *Imbrasia belina* are eaten by humans.

Similar species: Related to the Monkey Moths (family Eupterotidae), which lack eyespots.

Lappet or Eggar Moths

Bombycopsis, Eutricha, Pachypasa, Philotherma and others

Family: Lasiocampidae.

Average size: 5 cm wingspan.

Identification: Wings are usually mottled brown or orange-yellow. The hindwings are large and rounded, the forewings narrower, ending in a blunt point. The body is hairy and robust, the feelers are short and feathery in the male.

Distribution: Most of the 130 or so species occurring in the region are restricted to the northeastern parts of southern Africa. A few species are widespread.

Behaviour: Nocturnal[G], attracted to light. The male uses its feathery feelers to detect attractants released by the female.

Early stages: Eggs are laid in clusters. The caterpillars are large and flattened with long tufts of hair along their edges. The chrysalis[G] is contained in a tough silken cocoon, which is often covered in stinging hairs.

Opisthodontia sp.

Food: A wide range of families, including the Buffalo-thorn, Thorn-tree, Myrrh, Mango, Grass and Bauhinia families.

Notes: The family contains 50 genera. Adults do not feed. Some caterpillars are gregarious. Their stinging hairs cause skin irritation in humans.

Similar species: Prominent Moths (family Notodontidae).

Monkey Moths

Hemijana, Phiala, Phyllalia, Striphnopteryx and others

Family: Eupterotidae.

Average size: 7 cm wingspan.

Identification: Wings are usually mottled brown or orange-yellow; some moths are white with yellow bodies; the wings are large and rounded, and furry in appearance. The body is robust and hairy. The male has short, feathery feelers.

Distribution: Most of the 68 or so species occurring in the region are restricted to the northeastern parts of southern Africa; a few are restricted to the western Cape.

Behaviour: Nocturnal[G], attracted to light. The male uses its feathery feelers to detect attractants released by the female.

Early stages: Eggs are laid in clusters. The caterpillars are large with long black or orange hairs, often swept back. The chrysalis[G] is contained in an earthen cell.

Food: A wide range of families, including the Jacaranda, Forget-me-not, Coffee, Wild Elder, Grass and Bauhinia families.

Notes: The family contains 20 genera. The hairs on the caterpillars irritate the skin in humans.

Similar species: Related to the Emperor Moths (family Saturniidae), but lack the eyespots.

Striphnopteryx edulis

43

Looper Moths

Chiasmia, Heterorachis, Idaea, Neromia, Pingasa and others

Family: Geometridae.

Average size: 3-4 cm wingspan.

Identification: Wings are broad and the body is narrow. Wings are usually mottled brown, grey or white; some are brightly coloured green or orange.

Distribution: Many of the more than 1 000 described species occurring in the region are restricted to the northeastern parts of southern Africa. A number of these are widespread.

Behaviour: Adults are mostly nocturnal[G], attracted to light; flight is weak and fluttering. The moths rest with their wings spread flat against bark or leaves, blending into the background.

Early stages: The caterpillars are green or brown, slender and twig-like. They move by looping the body. The chrysalis[G] develops in silk or earthen cocoons underground or among leaves.

Food: A wide range of families, including the Thorn-tree, Tomato, Coffee, Cypress, Spike-thorn, Combretum, Mango and Bauhinia families.

Notes: The family contains 214 genera. The caterpillars resemble twigs, which provides camouflage.

Similar species: A few species mimic[G] the distasteful African Monarch Butterfly (family Nymphalidae; subfamily Danainae).

Pingasa distensaria

Hawk Moths

Acherontia, Cephonodes, Hippotion, Theretra and others

Family: Sphingidae.

Average size: 8 cm wingspan.

Identification: Wings of a few species are brightly coloured; often mottled brown or orange-yellow, narrow and streamlined. The body is robust with long, smooth feelers.

Distribution: Most of the 117 species occurring in the region are restricted to the northeastern parts of southern Africa; a few are restricted to the Western Cape.

Behaviour: Swift, powerful flyers. Nocturnal[G], and attracted to light. There are a few diurnal[G] species. Hawk Moths hover to extend their long tongues into flowers in search of nectar.

Early stages: Eggs are laid singly. The caterpillars are large, fat, and smooth with a horn on the rear end. They show a large false eye behind the head. The chrysalis[G] develops either under or above ground in loosely woven shelters of leaves.

Theretra caja

Food: A wide range of families, including the Fig, Elm, Jacaranda, Mango, Forget-me-not, Pea, Convolvulus, Bauhinia and Wild Elder families.

Notes: The family contains 49 genera. Hawk Moths can reach speeds of 50 km/h.

Similar species: Distinct from all other moths. The day-flying Oriental Bee Hawk (*Cephonodes hylas*) mimics[G] a large bee.

Prominent Moths

Afroplitis, Atrasana, Desmeocraera, Phalera and others

Family: Notodontidae (subfamilies: Notodontinae and Desmeocraerinae).

Average size: 8 cm wingspan.

Identification: Wings are mottled brown, yellow or green, though the hindwings are paler. There are a few white species. The forewings are narrow, and the hindwings broader and rounder. The body is large and hairy.

Distribution: Most of the approximately 175 species occurring in the region are restricted to the northeastern parts of southern Africa; a few are restricted to the western parts of the region.

Behaviour: Nocturnal[G], attracted to light. These moths rest on bark or among dried leaves for camouflage.

Early stages: The caterpillars are smooth or with sparse hairs; many have bizarre shapes, often with a hump behind the head. The chrysalis[G] develops in tough silken cocoons.

Food: A wide range of families, including the Fig, Bauhinia, Protea, Linden, Combretum and Guava families.

Notes: The family contains 82 genera. A tuft of scales on the edge of the forewing projects upwards when the wings are folded, giving rise to the common name.

Similar species: Lappet Moths (family Lasiocampidae).

Desmeocraera vernalis

46

Processionary Moths

Adrallia, Anaphe, Epanaphe, Thaumetopoea and others

Family: Notodontidae (subfamily: Thaumetopoeinae).

Average size: 4 cm wingspan.

Identification: Wings are usually white with a brown pattern on the forewings. The body is large and hairy.

Distribution: The six species occurring in the region are restricted to the northeastern parts of southern Africa.

Anaphe reticulata

Behaviour: The caterpillars are gregarious, sometimes wandering across the ground in single file, giving rise to the common name.

Early stages: The caterpillars are off-white and hairy. The chrysalis[G] develops in a silk cocoon. Several cocoons are cemented together in a tough outer bag of silk called a bagnest.

Food: Plants of the Oleander, Bauhinia, Cacao and Euphorbia families.

Notes: The family contains five genera. Up to 600 caterpillars may be found in a single bagnest.

Similar species: Similar in shape to some of the Lappet Moths (family Lasiocampidae) and Prominent Moths (family Notodontidae), but the markings are different.

Tussock Moths

Aroa, Euproctis, Lacipa, Lymantria, Psalis and others

Family: Lymantriidae.

Average size: 3,5 cm wingspan.

Identification: Wings are broad, usually yellow or white, sometimes mottled grey or brown. The body is usually hairy and robust, but may be slender; the feelers are fairly short.

Distribution: Most of the 158 or so species occurring in the region are restricted to the northeastern parts of southern Africa; a couple are restricted to the Western Cape of South Africa. A few are widespread.

Behaviour: Most are nocturnal[G], attracted to light, though there are a few diurnal[G] species. The adults do not feed.

Early stages: The caterpillars are often brightly coloured and hairy, frequently with upright brushes of hair on the back, giving rise to the common name. The chrysalis[G] is contained in a silk cocoon.

Lacipa pulverea

Food: A wide range of families including the Fig, Daisy, Hibiscus, Bauhinia, Thorn-tree, Grass, Mango and Combretum families.

Notes: The family contains 45 genera. Hairs from the caterpillars may irritate the skin, causing rashes.

Similar species: May be confused with the Owl Moths (family Noctuidae) and the Prominent Moths (family Notodontidae).

Handmaiden Moths

Asinusca, Cacosoma, Euchromia, Eutomis, Syntomis and others

Family: Arctiidae (subfamily Ctenuchinae).

Average size: 2,5 cm wingspan.

Identification: Wings are usually black with white transparent patches, sometimes marked yellow, and narrow; the hind-wing is small. The abdomen often has red stripes; the feelers are long and thin.

Distribution: Most of the 52 species occurring in the region are restricted to the northeastern parts of southern Africa. A few are widespread.

Behaviour: Mostly diurnal[G]; slow flying, often settling on vegetation.

Early stages: The caterpillars are short and round with tufts of long hair. The chrysalis[G] develops in a silk cocoon.

Food: Plants of the Coffee, Grass, Convolvulus and Oleander families.

Notes: The family contains 10 genera. Wasp-like banding on the abdomen, and together with the narrow wings suggest they mimic[G] wasps.

Similar species: Closely related to the Tiger Moths (family Arctiidae), but often confused with the more primitive Burnets (family Zygaenidae).

Syntomis kuhlweini

Tiger Moths

Amerila, Chiromachla, Estigmene, Rhodogastria and others

Family: Arctiidae (subfamily: Arctiinae).

Average size: 4,5 cm wingspan.

Identification: Wings are usually narrow and brightly coloured white or yellow with black or red markings. The body is robust; the feelers are long and thin.

Distribution: Most of the approximately 102 species occurring in the region are restricted to the northeastern parts of southern Africa. A few are widespread.

Behaviour: Most are nocturnal[G], attracted to light; a few are diurnal[G]. These moths feign death when handled or threatened.

Early stages: Eggs are laid singly or in clusters. The caterpillars are usually very hairy. The chrysalis[G] develops in a thin silken cocoon.

Food: A wide range of families including the Daisy, Coffee, Jacaranda, Tomato, Mango and Bauhinia families.

Notes: The subfamily contains 40 genera. Caterpillars are hairy, popularly called 'woolly bears'. The bright colours of the adult and some caterpillars warn predators that they are distasteful.

Similar species: Snouted Tiger Moths (family Arctiidae; subfamily Aganainae), False Tiger Moths (family Agaristidae).

Rhodogastria amasis

Snouted Tiger Moths

Psephea

Family: Aganaidae.

Average size: 4-5 cm wingspan.

Identification: Wings are orange with brown and black markings; the forewings are narrow. The body is fairly slender and the feelers are long and thin. The head has prominent palps[G], giving rise to the common name.

Psephea speciosa

Distribution: The three species occurring in the region are restricted to the northeastern parts of southern Africa. *Psephea speciosa* has been introduced to the Western Cape.

Behaviour: Nocturnal[G], attracted to light. These moths feign death when handled or threatened.

Early stages: The caterpillars may be brightly coloured; they are covered with sparse hairs. The chrysalis[G] is contained within a thin silken cocoon.

Food: Plants in the Fig and Oleander families.

Notes: The family contains one genus. Four other genera, previously included in the family Aganaidae, have recently been moved to the family Noctuidae. The bright colours of the adults and caterpillars warn predators of their distastefulness.

Similar species: Tiger Moths (family Arctiidae; subfamily Arctiinae), False Tiger Moths (family Noctuidae, subfamily Agaristinae).

False Tiger Moths

Aegoceropsis, Brephos, Heraclia, Ovios, Rothia and others

Family: Noctuidae (subfamily Agaristinae)

Average size: 4,5 cm wingspan.

Identification: Wings are usually brightly coloured: black, yellow and red, or black, yellow and white. The body is slender and hairy, the feelers long and thin.

Distribution: Most of the 30 species occurring in the region are restricted to the northeastern parts of southern Africa. A few are widespread.

Behaviour: Most species are diurnal[G]. These moths fly swiftly, often settling abruptly on vegetation.

Early stages: The caterpillars are usually brightly coloured and hairy.

Food: A number of plant families, including the Grape, Coffee and Protea families.

Notes: Males of some species often make a rattling noise in flight. The moths' bright colours act as a warning to predators. The family contains 19 genera.

Similar species: Tiger Moths (family Arctiidae; subfamily Arctiinae) and Snouted Tiger Moths (family Aganaidae).

Heraclia superba

Owl Moths

Agrotis, Autoba, Centrartha, Heliothis, Lycophotia and others

Family: Noctuidae.

Average size: 4 cm wingspan.

Identification: Wings are usually drab, with mottled grey or brown forewings and pale hindwings. There are a few brightly coloured species. The body is usually robust and hairy, the feelers long and slender.

Autoba costimacula

Distribution: A number of the more than 2 000 described species occurring in the region are restricted to the northeastern parts of southern Africa. Many are widespread.

Behaviour: Mostly nocturnal[G], attracted to light; there are a few diurnal[G] species.

Early stages: The caterpillars are usually green or brown, often striped; their bodies are smooth and hairless, a few are hairy, or have long paddle-shaped filaments. The chrysalis[G] is usually formed in a fragile earthen or silk cocoon, often just below ground level.

Food: Plants of an extremely wide range of families including many agricultural crops.

Notes: Largest family of Lepidoptera; contains 427 genera.

Similar species: May be confused with Tussock Moths (family Lymantriidae).

Glossary

Abdomen: The third, last section of the body after the thorax.
Chrysalis: The inactive stage in the life cycle when the caterpillar changes into an adult.
Diurnal: Active during the day.
Endemic: A species whose range is confined to a specific region.
Keel: Projecting to a sharp edge.
Metamorphosis: The process of change from a caterpillar to an adult moth or butterfly.
Mimic: Superficial resemblance of a moth or butterfly species to another species of moth or butterfly that is distasteful or that has irritating hairs, in order to discourage predators.
Nocturnal: Active at night.
Palps: Jointed feelers originating from the lower lip or jaw.
Polymorphic: Presence of a number of different forms.
Thorax: The second, middle section of the body from which the legs and wings arise.
Wing cases: Area of the chrysalis covering the developing wings.

Brush-footed Butterfly, *Junonia hierta*

Recommended further reading

Henning, G.A., Henning, S.F., Joannou, J.G. & Woodhall, S.E. 1997. *Living Butterflies of Southern Africa. Biology, Ecology and Conservation.* Umdaus Press, Hatfield.

Henning, S.F., Henning, G.A. 1989. *South African Red Data Book – Butterflies.* South African National Scientific Programmes Report No. 158, Foundation for Research and Development, CSIR, Pretoria.

Janse, A.J.T. 1932-1964. *The Moths of South Africa.* Vol. I-VII. Pretoria, Transvaal Museum.

Migdoll, I. 1987. *Field Guide to the Butterflies of Southern Africa.* Struik (Pty) Ltd, Cape Town.

Oberprieler, R. 1995. *The Emperor Moths of Namibia.* Ecoguild, Hartebeespoort.

Pinhey, E.C.G. 1962. *Hawk Moths of Central and Southern Africa.* Longmans (Pty) Ltd, Cape Town.

Pinhey, E.C.G. 1972. *Emperor Moths of South and South Central Africa.* Struik (Pty) Ltd, Cape Town.

Pinhey, E.C.G. 1975. *Moths of Southern Africa.* Tafelberg, Cape Town.

Pinhey, E.C.G. 1975. *Some Well Known*

Tussock Moth, *Knappetra fasciata*

African Moths. Bundu Series, Longmans (Pty) Ltd, Salisbury.

Pringle, E.L.L., Henning G.A. & Ball, J.B. (eds.) 1994. *Pennington's Butterflies of Southern Africa.* Second Edition. Struik Winchester, Cape Town.

Williams, M. 1994. *Butterflies of Southern Africa. A Field Guide.* Southern Book Publishers, Halfway House.

Woodhall, S.E. (ed.) 1992. *A Practical Guide to Butterflies and Moths in Southern Africa.* The Lepidopterist's Society of Southern Africa, Florida Hills.

Index and checklist

Acraea Butterflies 16 ☐
Bagworm Moths 31 ☐
Blue Butterflies 28 ☐
Brown Butterflies 18 ☐
Brush-footed Butterflies 19 ☐
Burnet Moths 35 ☐
Charaxes Butterflies 20 ☐
Clearwing Moths 33 ☐
Clothes Moths 32 ☐
Copper Butterflies 25 ☐
Emperor Moths 41 ☐
False Tiger Moths 52 ☐
Ghost Moths 30 ☐
Goat Moths 34 ☐
Grass Yellow Butterflies 14 ☐
Hairtail Butterflies 27 ☐
Handmaiden Moths 49 ☐
Hawk Moths 45 ☐
Lappet or Eggar Moths 42 ☐
Leaf Rolling Moths 36 ☐
Looper Moths 44 ☐
Monarch Butterflies 17 ☐
Monkey Moths 43 ☐
Opal Butterflies 26 ☐
Orange Tip Butterflies 15 ☐
Owl Moths 53 ☐
Purple Tip Butterflies 15 ☐
Pearl Moths 38 ☐
Plume Moths 39 ☐
Processionary Moths 47 ☐

Bag of Bagworm Moth

Prominent Moths 46 ☐
Sapphire Butterflies 24 ☐
Silk Moths 40 ☐
Skipper Butterflies 29 ☐
Skolly Butterflies 23 ☐
Slug Moths 37 ☐
Snout Butterflies 21 ☐
Snouted Tiger Moths 51 ☐
Swallowtail Butterflies 10 ☐
Swordtail Butterflies 11 ☐
Tiger Moths 50 ☐
Tussock Moths 48 ☐
Vagrant Butterflies 13 ☐
White Butterflies 12 ☐
Zulu Butterflies 22 ☐